HOMME

MASTERPIECES OF EROTIC PHOTOGRAPHY

D1289228

THIS IS A CARLTON BOOK

Design copyright © 1999 Carlton Books Limited
Text copyright © 1999 Carlton Books Limited

This edition published by Carlton Books Limited 2000
20 Mortimer Street
London
W1N 7RD

This book is sold subject to the condition that it shall not, by way of trade or otherwise, be lent, resold, hired out or otherwise circulated without the publisher's prior written consent in any form of cover or binding other than that in which it is published and without a similar condition including this condition, being imposed upon the subsequent purchaser.

All rights reserved.

A CIP catalogue for this book is available
from the British Library.

ISBN 1 85868 847 7

Reprinted 2000

Design: ADAM WRIGHT
Picture research: ALEX PEPPER
Production: ALEXIA TURNER

Printed in Spain.

HOMME

MASTERPIECES OF EROTIC PHOTOGRAPHY

MICHELLE OLLEY

CARLTON

CONTENTS PAGE

INTRODUCTION

If you want evidence that the world we now live in has changed forever, you need look no further than the imagery that surrounds us in fashion, art, film and music. Things are hotting up. 'Sexy' is no longer an adjective strictly for the girls. Men are getting in on the act. Modern ideas of beauty and sexuality have evolved to match our new, hard-won values of equality, honesty and increased artistic freedom. Nowhere is this more apparent than in the depiction of the male nude. The history of the twentieth century's changing attitudes towards the body, towards sexual diversity, and towards women are revealed in the changing images of masculinity captured on film by successive eras of the century's major new art form – photography. Brave pioneer photographers who have dared to push back the boundaries of what can be revealed have helped to shape the cultural landscape we now live in. What these photographs of male nudes reveal goes far deeper than mere anatomy. They reveal men's and women's evolving place in the world. They reveal a society coming to terms with its citizens' desires and learning not to fear them.

"Sex", as Gore Vidal noted in 1979, "is politics." The threat of the moral breakdown of western society and sexual and civil anarchy if the family ideal was not rigorously upheld, has kept the policing of the public's sexual mores a priority for hundreds, nay thousands, of years. The Christian church viewed sexuality, particularly women's, as something potentially explosive and uncontrollable, capable of leading mankind into serious sin. Sex had to be controlled and kept to its reproductive function. Marriage was the only acceptable platform for the expression of desire and a convenient way to provide new, legitimate citizens. Homosexuality and promiscuity were considered abominations, and nudity was stripped of its innocence by original sin: knowledge brought awareness of nudity, and with it shame, into the garden of Eden. Also, for the early Christian ideology to take hold, the old ways had to be discredited. Pagan religions, with their strong matriarchal ties to nature, birth, fertility and magical rituals, sometimes involving nudity, were often portrayed as debauched and impure. Sex and desire became pregnant with sin – only the weak succumbed to earthly temptation.

Early western Christian society's fear of sexual arousal through the display or depiction of the body did not stop artists from finding a way around this problem, though. They simply incorporated the nude into religious or classical compositions based on the sculptures and artifacts of ancient Greece and Rome. Pre-Christian art, particularly that of the Romans and the Greeks, celebrated the male nude figure as the location of the sexual ideal, more so than the female nude, who often appeared draped in flowing robes. Ancient Greek society celebrated athleticism and encouraged 'mentor' relationships between young men and older soldiers and athletes, as these relationships were thought to strengthen the loyalty and camaraderie of the warrior class. A love of the male figure carried no taboo for these societies. After the fall of Rome and the rise of Christianity, the artistic tradition of studying form and male anatomy was able to flower again during the Renaissance, when Michelangelo's religious works came to the fore. Other artists followed suit, and the male nude enjoyed a return to favour, if only within the confines of mythological or religious scenarios. Often though, the nude figures in art during the seventeenth, eighteenth and particularly the nineteenth century were women, depicted as goddesses and nymphs. Naked men were still perceived as vulnerable and emasculated and therefore not so in demand.

When photography arrived on the scene, during the Victorian period, the compulsion to cover up the human figure was at an almost hysterical level. Amongst high society, women's day dresses went from neck to floor, though tightly bound at the waist to emphasise femininity and fragility. Men were encumbered in long, heavy suits, cravats, spats, gloves and hats. Even the table legs in Victorian parlours had to be covered up with swathes of fabric, for the sake of modesty. Naturally enough, the human erotic impulse could not be entirely submerged in all that fabric. The female nude in art was as popular as ever, particularly with the newly-wealthy industrialists, who were rapidly marrying into the old aristocracy, and who were becoming the main collectors of erotic art. Underground erotic photography fitted comfortably into this market and began almost as soon as the camera appeared. "What The Butler Saw" pictures, particularly the Butler who travelled to the brothels of Paris, were soon making their appearance in the racier salons of Victorian society. Despite having a woman on the throne, men very much made the rules. Married women at this time were not allowed to own or inherit property, had no rights over their children and were not allowed to vote, and to be unmarried was grievous. Homosexuality was made an imprisonable offence for men during Victoria's reign (she famously

refused to outlaw female homosexuality as she could not see how it could be possible), so photographs of naked men had to be presented with extreme care.

The first photographic images drew on the 'classical' tradition of male beauty. They depicted strongmen like the famous Eugene Sandow, who flexed his muscles for the camera in 1890. The education of artists provided an early legitimate avenue for exploring the male form. Male nude anatomy photographs began to be produced for artists who could not afford to work with live models. Eadweard Muybridge took the study of movement forward when he devised a technique for capturing movement by using a sequence of cameras.

At the beginning of the twentieth century, the Greek idyll began to appear on camera. Photographers like Baron Wilhelm von Gloeden began taking pictures of local Sicilian boys dressed in togas, which did a roaring trade with the visiting tourists. In Europe, "natural" photography was gaining a following. The athletic male, enjoying sunshine and sporting pursuits, already had a place in fine art. After the First World War, this celebration of athleticism and fitness became more prominent. Suddenly, the constricted, stuffy heirs to the Victorians and Edwardians wanted out of their stays and waistcoats. Fashions in the 1920s

and '30s began to loosen up. Magazines like *Physical Culture* and *Vim* (later to become *Health and Efficiency*) promoted a new celebration of the body, in a strictly non-sexual sense, of course. Naturism became the new cause célèbre, particularily in Scandinavia.

The worlds of dance and theatre and the emerging Hollywood stars brought new opportunities for photographers to portray the male figure and reach a new audience of male and female admirers. By the 1930s, photography was beginning to establish its credentials as a serious artform. Artists like Man Ray in Paris and Cecil Beaton in Hollywood were beginning to use light and developing techniques to create images of great beauty. Soon, the depiction of the male figure would become less coy. Pioneers like George Platt Lynes built up an impressive portfolio of naked male images in the forties and fifties, along with his successful fashion work. Often, Platt Lynes would shoot these images after a long day shooting 'regular' fashion, using the same sets. Although his nude work was rarely seen in its day, he is now considered one of the seminal artists working in this field.

Wars have a habit of changing everything. Whilst interest in erotic art photography was growing slowly through the 1920s, with little change through the 1930s, it was the Second

World War which really started to break down the barriers of prudishness. Old ideas about morality and sexuality were being put under pressure; the threat of destruction can bring priorities into sharp focus, as can travel away from the family hearth. After the war, a new, more sophisticated generation of men who knew they were never going to marry appeared. The old health and fitness oriented magazines gave way to a new wave of publications which presented gleaming, muscle-bound torsos for the appreciative eye. Magazines like *Physique Pictorial* and UK-based photographer John Barrington's *Male Model Monthly* made no attempt to pass themselves off as fitness guides. They even had biographies of the models' hobbies and interests – a charming precursor to the way traditional "glamour" models are presented now.

But it took the rock and roll rebellion of the 1950s and the sexual revolution of the 1960s to really shake things up. Without Elvis and his pelvis, without the hippies and their advocacy of free sexual expression, without the civil liberties movements advocating women's and gay rights, and without the artists and photographers who seized the opportunity to express that moral wind-change through their work, we would never have progressed to the point we find ourselves at

now. After so many years of moral censure, sexuality and the depiction of the body was becoming liberated. The baby boomers – children born after the Second World War, rebelled against the traditional suburban family values that they were brought up with. There was a whole new, Technicolor, prosperous world out there and people wanted to get groovy.

As old gender roles broke down, the macho hunk no longer represented the male beauty ideal. Skinny-hipped, long-haired rock stars, with barely the muscle to lift a microphone stand, let alone weights, became the new sex gods. Women lost their sculpted, artificial curves and became natural "child-women" (in theory – in reality, for most women, the child-woman took as much work to achieve as the curvy 'fifties "dame", the skinny 'twenties "flapper", or the 'eighties "hardbody", but that is body fashion for you). Thanks to the new climate, in the 1970s it became possible for women like Dianora Niccolini to be taken seriously as photographers of male nudes.

It was during the 1980s that the male figure really began to realise its full potential in the field of photography. After years of being consigned to the obscurity of "beefcake" magazines or small interest high art works, in the 1980s the erotic power of the male nude was finally

realised. There are a number of reasons for this, but timing is the main one. Not only was photographic technology reaching its apex, but the generation who grew up in the 'sixties, inspired by their times and by the work that had come before them, were also coming to the fore, These photographers were not encumbered by outdated ideas about what was or was not permissible. There was no longer any shame in portraying the male nude, because there was no longer any shame in creating desire or admiration for him. Officially, the sophisticated western world no longer depended on male domination and female submission to function. And thanks to pioneering works in the medical field (take a bow Dr Kinsey, take a bow Dr Ruth!), we understand the importance and benefits of sexual fantasy.

Robert Mapplethorpe was the pioneer here, along with Annie Leibovitz's rock portraits, Bruce Weber's and Herb Ritts's stunning monochrome fashion work and Greg Gorman's sculpted portraiture. This was the moment when mass culture and advertising caught up with the prevailing trend. Just as the female pin-up had been seized upon in the 'sixties and 'seventies to sell everything from rum to car tyres, hunky male bodies were drafted in to seduce the female consumer into buying luxury goods, from cosmetics to premium ice-cream. The 'eighties poster hunk, cradling the baby or straddling a motorbike, marked a new era in male beauty, and represented the pinnacle of gym-toned perfection, if you like that sort of thing – and millions of us did. In art and fashion photography, sexual imagery was taking a turn for the better – strong, assertive, intelligent, up-front glamour was replacing classical, more passive poses. Male models, for the first time, were becoming stars.

The explosion of high-octane hyper-glamourous imagery continued into the late 1990s, when a new style of photography emerged. New photographers were moving the emphasis away from the body and towards the bigger picture. Perhaps due to the strong influence of fashion photography – always the most directional of photographic genres – the scenario and the model's personality are now coming to the fore. This is true of both male and female imagery: context has never been more important or more intruiging. The new photographers coming through who use the naked image as part of a more complex narrative are taking the male nude into a whole new area, as far from the fig leaves and Greek urns as you can get. Ultra-real home environments like Terry Richardson's, the club environments of Alex Gerry and the urban landscapes of Jay Eff place the male figure in his own timeframe. New photographic techniques, like David Zanes' individual Polaroid images, give a timeless quality via a thoroughly modern look, whilst elaborate fantasy worlds, like the ones created by Pierre et Gilles, send us back to the dream state. And finally, more body types are proliferating throughout art and fashion. The smooth, sculpted 'Adonis' hunk is being joined by a band of skinnier, hairier, more diverse men and boys.

Thanks to the work of many great photographers and artists, the male nude has arrived at the end of the twentieth century with his dignity pretty much intact. The best figurative imagery, no matter how far it goes, always contains an inherent respect for and collaboration with the model. The modern nude is the subject, not the object. The idea that a naked male image disempowers not only the man in the image but the man viewing it, and therefore all males, has thankfully been consigned to the dustbin of history, along with other outdated ideas. Looking at how far we have come in the past thirty years, one only hopes that this trend continues, and that the narrow definitions of beauty that women have suffered under and struggled to release themselves from do not start to afflict men. A six-pack isn't everything you know, boys.

In choosing the images for this book we have attempted to give some sort of overview to this diverse genre of photography. As is often the case with these kind of publications, it has been difficult to narrow it down to just under 200 photographs. We have included a little bit of history, some seminal images you may be familiar with, some big names and some new names who we think you will be hearing a lot more from. Some of the most stunning and the most challenging work being done today is coming from the world of fashion photography, and both the aspirational and the new verité styles are represented here. Every photographer who has kindly agreed to inclusion in this book has something unique to offer. We hope that this anthology intrigues, thrills and delights anyone who comes across it. In this day and age, we are all intelligent enough to see that the human form is a thing of beauty, to be celebrated in whatever artform we see fit, as indeed mankind has been doing since the dawn of time. With computer technology proceeding apace, who knows where photography in the twenty-first century will take us. One thing is for sure though, as long as we have free will and equality, the artist's curiosity about man's (and woman's) essential beauty will continue to take centre stage.

THE PHOTOGRAPHERS

MICHAEL BAUMGARTEN

We have *Attitude* magazine's ever-vigilant fashion director Adrian Clark to thank for this special discovery. Michael Baumgarten is a sizzle-hot new name in fashion photography, based in Paris, and currently working with, amongst others, *Attitude* and French *Vogue*. His male nudes have not been published before, but it can only be a matter of time before his beautiful images become sought after by fans of this emerging genre. Baumgarten got into photography through the dues-paying route of assisting on shoots in Paris and building up an impressive portfolio of personal work. One to watch.

RICK CASTRO

Castro's work incorporates both photography and film. The auteur behind the critically acclaimed underground movie *Hustler White*, (starring Madonna's and the Spice Girls' video-romping partner Tony Ward, featured here), has been using his camera to document beauty wherever he finds it, which includes some interesting places – the aesthetic appeal of Japanese rope bondage (as seen in his range of Bondage Books), the inner world of fetishists and cross-dressers, and the culture of male prostitution – hustling. Not afraid to shed light into new areas, Castro is currently working on a movie that will be "a black comedy – a lesbian epic about all the pre-Stonewall melodramas up to and including the 'sixties...".

MICHAEL CHILDERS

Renowned Hollywood-based celebrity photographer Michael Childers is one of the stars of this anthology. Instrumental in creating the early images of Mel Gibson, Demi Moore, Richard Gere and John Travolta, he was a founding photographer for Andy Warhol's *Interview* magazine and remains at the forefront of his field today. Childers' images reflect his cinematographic heritage (he was a graduate from UCLA film school), combining erotically charged scenarios with larger-than-life Hollywood glamour. Don't you wish your life was like a Childers photograph?

DOUGLAS CLOUTIER

One of the founders of seminal male nude art/photography bible, *Provocateur* magazine, Douglas Cloutier has built up an outstanding portfolio of both male and female erotic images. There's something heroic and strong about many of Cloutier's photographs. A master of lighting and contrast, Cloutier's work sometimes draws from the classic poses of art and statuary, breathing new life into traditional shapes, and sometimes uses nature to frame his figures to bold effect. This Hollywood-based photographer's work is collected together in a beautiful anthology called simply, *Douglas Cloutier* (Alluvial Press).

IAN DAVID BAKER

Photography is not the only medium at the disposal of this Renaissance man. Ian David Baker has also successfully put his hand to graphic design, fine art drawing, journalism, editing, DJ-ing, singing in a blues band and even, for four years in the early 'nineties, working as a newsreader and music presenter on English language radio in Bangkok and Thailand. Now London based, and concentrating on his photography and painting, Baker's male nudes display the same sensitivity and romantic quality that critics have ascribed to his fine art work.

JAY EFF

One of the most popular photographers on the London club scene, Jay Eff's striking hand-painted images of drop-dead gorgeous muscle boys set against Technicolor urban environments have made collectable artworks out of club flyers (particularly for the Heaven nightclub) for a large part of the 'nineties. Also featured on the book jackets of fantasy writer Christopher Fowler, Eff's work captures the vibrancy of London's boy beautiful tribe. For this anthology, we chose to feature some of Eff's less-known reportage portraiture – former Mr Gay UK, the divine Mr Mark Anthony, is captured between shows on his UK tour. Male beauty in the raw.

ROBERT FLYNT

The beautiful images of Robert Flynt combine photography and art to create images that seem to come from the past and yet are entirely new. These Chromogenic prints and Cibachromes mix ancient and modern scenes, often incorporating water, sometimes superimposing graphics from wrestling or lifeguard manuals into the scenario. Flynt's images seem to occupy some other-worldly space, where men swim, float and entwine with each other, oblivious to their everyday surroundings. One for all those wannabe water babies.

ALEX GERRY

London-based photographer and writer Gerry has been cataloguing the misadventures of club people since 1989, building up a breathtaking portfolio of images, which have been published in all the right magazines from DJ and Mixmag to the Evening Standard and the Independent. Getting a great shot in a smoky, crowded nightclub is a real skill, and Gerry is a consummate expert. Male beauty is everywhere in clubland, if you know where to look, and Gerry knows exactly where to find it. He is currently writing a history of clubland and clubpeople to accompany his outstanding collection of images, with a view to publishing a book in the not-too-distant future.

BARON WILHELM von GLOEDEN (1856-1931)

One of the first photographers ever to feature the male nude, von Gloeden avoided the prurient attitudes of his times by recreating the ancient Greek idyll. His images of Sicilian local boys in togas and laurel wreaths were sold as postcards to tourists in the area. Although this Prussian-born aristocrat's work was originally dismissed as kitsch, it has undergone reappraisal in recent years. Von Gloeden's classic poses can be seen reflected in the work of artists as diverse as Robert Mapplethorpe and Pierre et Gilles.

NAN GOLDIN

Taking a walk on the wild, side of New York's artistic underground is an act of love for Nan Goldin. Her intimate images of friends and lovers, taken during the Big Apple's heady party years of the 1970s and '80s go behind the public personas of the characters who 'made the scene'. There is a vulnerability and nakedness about some of Goldin's images which suggests a level of closeness with her subjects rarely seen in photography. Poignantly, too many of Goldin's friends died young, early victims of the AIDS epidemic: "I used to think that I could never lose anyone if I photographed them enough. In fact, my pictures show me how many I've lost." Books published include *The Ballad of Sexual Dependency* (Aperture) and *The Other Side* (Scalo).

GREG GORMAN

You are nobody in Hollywood until you have been shot by this man. Greg Gorman is one of portrait photography's major players. He has photographed the biggest stars on the planet – from Bette Davis to David Bowie; some of his major ad campaigns have been for the likes of Coca-Cola and Canon; and he has directed numerous music videos and TV advertisements. Currently working on a collection of his portraits and nudes from 1968–96, this LA-based photographer's work can also be found in two anthologies – *Greg Gorman Volume One* (CPC Publishing) and *Volume Two* (Treville Press).

BALY HINTER WIPFLINGER

After a successful career making marble and bronze statues for architects and antique dealers and modelling for the likes of Andy Warhol and Greg Gorman, this talented photographer began creating the images for himself in 1992. What began as a hobby soon bloomed into a vocation, as Wipflinger's exquisite black and white work was seized on by galleries and publishers who were suitably impressed. His influences – Wilhelm von Gloeden and Robert Mapplethorpe – are given a modern twist by Wipflinger's talent for bringing lightness and wit to his work. No wonder Elton John is said to be a fan.

HORST P. HORST

Along with Cecil Beaton and Man Ray, Horst is one of the leading fashion and society portrait photographers of the pre and post-war years. Horst began his career studying architecture in Hamburg and Paris but after a stint as a model for French *Vogue's* chief photographer in 1930, George Hoyningen-Heune, he soon switched to the other side of the camera and became his pupil. Horst began working for *Vogue* soon after, emigrating to the USA in 1935. Horst's work often has an epic quality to it – his use of props and blown up backgrounds and his expert use of light give his images a classic cinematic feel.

JAMES & JAMES

London-based photographic partnership James Green and James Stafford have been at the forefront of the new generation of fetish fashion crossover photography since the early 'nineties. Their use of bright colour and creative Photoshop image manipulation has brought a fresh look to the fetish genre. For this book, we chose a selection of their fashion and portraiture work, including images from fetish couture label House of Harlot and portraits of poet and porn star Aiden Shaw and the pervy prince of pop, Marc Almond.

STEPHEN JEFFERY-POULTER (SJP)

It is hard to believe that London-based Stephen Jeffery-Poulter took up male figure photography only three years ago, finding his work accepted for publication six months later. There's a refreshingly brazen sensuality and beauty to Jeffery-Poulter's images that may be due to his choice of models and location: "The majority of my models have never done nude work before, which, I believe, brings a freshness and variety to the results. Whenever possible I use natural light and prefer to shoot out of doors – although that's always a battle given the vagaries of the English summer!" You can see more of Jeffery-Poulter's work at: www.homoerotica.co.uk

SANDRA JENSEN

"Photography for me is to get lost in a dream. I create my own world where anything can happen." When it comes to creating worlds, this Norwegian/Polish 24-year-old has been busier than most. From her Oslo-based Black Factory Studio, she runs her own modelling agency, shot five short films and two movies which she directed, scripted, edited and also did the make-up and costumes, as well as some of the acting. But photography is Sandra Jensen's first love. Her work is undeniably sensual – her f. Ex Radio Tango ad was chosen by *French Photo* as one of the sexiest ads of the year. She is currently working with erotic nouveau fashion magazine *Pure*.

JEANETTE JONES

Describing herself as "just an Essex housewife who took evening classes to learn how to take pictures", Jones began her photographic career documenting the burgeoning drag/cross-dressing scene in London and New York in the late 'eighties and early 'nineties, collected together in her book *A Walk on the Wild Side* (Souvenir Press). Between the drag clubs, Jones began shooting more masculine physiques, and is now one of our best-known and best-loved "male glamour" photographers. Jones's love of natural light and instinctive eye for a sexy shot has created some of the most delightful images in the genre, proving that it is not just the girls who can get glamorous.

DEAN KEEFER

For Dean Keefer, it is all about "the captured moment". While captured images of male beauty may be what first grabs the eye, it is Keefer's playful use of narrative that keeps the viewers coming back for more. Male pin-up imagery of this high standard is not easy to pull off. But it is easy to see why this quiet and unassuming gentleman is one of the most published male nude photographers in the world, producing many of the iconic posters, cards and calendars available today. His client list includes such notables as Boeing Aircraft, Universal Studios and *Playgirl* magazine, and is regularly shown in galleries around the world.

RICHARD KERN

Beginning his career as New York bad boy par excellence, Kern picked up impeccable underground credentials as one of the instigators of the "Cinema of Transgression", an edgy, nihilistic, sometimes violent genre which had as many detractors as admirers. Pushing the boundaries on and off screen eventually led to Kern having to quit New York, returning to photography to shoot his gun-metal cool *New York Girls* series (published by Taschen). Although drawn mostly to documenting the female urban hipster, along the way Kern has also turned his well-trained eye to some of the sassy boys who have got that same switched-on Manhattan street life glamour going on.

DORIS KLOSTER

Bringing a hefty slab of New York cool to the proceedings, the work of Doris Kloster oozes suss and attitude. Part of the team who produce cutting-edge US style mag *Fad*, Kloster's work has always been at the archer end of glamour. Probably best known for her delicious fashion work and her portraits of Manhattan dominatrixes, some of it featured in her first book, *Doris Kloster* (Taschen), the images featured here of men hanging out in the meat market are typical of Kloster's sexy, irreverent take on the world, as seen in her second book *Forms of Desire* (St Martin's Press), which features many more exotic denizens of the sexual underworld.

ROB LANG

The desert forms the backdrop for this New York-based photographer's male nude work. Shooting against the stunning landscapes and vistas of White Sands, New Mexico, Lang's background in sculpture and art helps to give these images their painterly feel. Often the aim in these images is to bring together the model and the landscape to create something new. Lang puts this beautifully in *Blue* magazine #19; "They're standing around naked in the desert and I have to get them connected to something beyond what they think and what they feel. But once they get there, the best pictures are the ones that they create themselves, that I simply capture."

GRACE LAU

One of the founder members of *Skin Two* magazine, London-based Lau was the first woman to document London's emerging fetish scene in the early 1980s. An academic and determined feminist, she was attracted to the way the scene promoted the idea of empowerment – both for women and men, submissives and dominants – and her early black and white work set out to capture that on film. As time went on Lau became particularly interested in photographing men in the SM and crossdressing scenes, as well as in the idea of women's reactions to men in sexual situations, such as male stripping. Some of the results of this investigation are published here.

EDWARD LUCIE-SMITH

Art historian and photographer Edward Lucie-Smith has a clear understanding of the dynamics of the male nude. In his excellent study *Adam, The Male Figure in Art*, (Weidenfeld & Nicolson), Lucie-Smith tracks the development of the artist's struggle to depict the male figure within the confines of their society. Lucie-Smith's soft-focus black-and-white photography concentrates on the beauty and vulnerability of the male form, without in any way emasculating the subject. You can almost sink into these images.

PIERRE MARCAR

No stranger to capturing the beauty of man and nature, London-based poet and photographer Marcar's soulful images of the human form in settings of natural beauty turn up on a wide range of posters and cards. The two images chosen for this anthology were taken in northern France, using a model who had never posed nude before. They serve as great examples of Marcar's mastery of the use of natural light and colour.

MICHELE MARTINOLI

Swiss-born, London-based photographer Michele Martinoli not only has a talent for producing images of beautiful men, she can create the men too – the Adonis featured here is her son! Martinoli specializes in fashion, portraiture and body shots. In the past four years she has become a regular contributor to London's leading gay magazines, *OX, Boyz, Diva, Axiom Health* and Australia's *Blue*, along with her regular fashion agency and music work. That her images can be seen displayed prominently at several bars across the capital, including Soho's The Village and The Yard, is testament to her popularity.

DAVID MORGAN

This New York-based photographer started out as an actor, taking pictures while on the road as a way to pass the time. Theatres need photographers with an eye for a striking image, and Morgan soon found himself shooting his first male nude, for a production of Noel Coward's *Anything Goes*. Morgan's theatre work led to a number of seminal club flyers through 1991–92, including an image of seven gym boys dancing together for Bruce Mailman's White Party. These bold and beautiful images, along with several fashion jobs, have gone on to establish Morgan as one of New York's key documenters of 'nineties male strength and beauty.

MARK MORRISROE

Like Nan Goldin and Jack Pierson, Morrisroe was a member of a group of photographers known as the Boston School. Morrisroe's short but colourful life threatens to overshadow his work. Morrisroe was born to a drug-addict prostitute mother, and claimed to be the progeny of the Boston Strangler; he moved into prostitution at 13, before giving it up around age 17 and going to art school. His main body of photographic work is his journalistic collection of Polaroids, taken with the 195 Land camera – self-portraits, or images of friends taken in New York between 1977 and his death from an AIDS-related illness in 1989. Like Goldin, there's a gentle, candid intimacy to these images. Moving, revealing work.

DIANORA NICCOLINI

One of the first women to enter the field of male nude photography, the influence of Dianora Niccolini should not be underestimated. Taking up the camera after a chance meeting with Weegee in 1963, her exhibition of male nude images in 1975 (including an African-American body-builder – predating Mapplethorpe by several years) caused a storm in the art world. Concentrating the gaze on the body, Niccolini's work celebrates the perfection of the human form. This New York-based artist and photographer was the first president of the Professional Women Photographers group, which she served for five years.

RICHARD PHIBBS

No-one captures the pioneer spirit of America quite like Richard Phibbs. This Calgary-born fashion and travel photographer, who regularly shoots for *Interview* and *Vanity Fair*, modestly sees his role as being "to capture the beauty that is already there…". That is beauty that comes from simplicity, not fashion artifice. But not everybody can turn a Coney Island mechanic into an Adonis. That is Phibbs' magic. No wonder Ralph Lauren chose him to shoot the TV and magazine ad campaigns for their all-American Polo range. You can find more of Phibbs' work in *Naked Flowers Exposed* (HarperCollins), a photographic anthology in aid of the Friends in Deed charity.

PIERRE ET GILLES

This Paris-based partnership have been responsible for some of the most colourful and flamboyant photography of the past two decades. Their flair for fantasy and brighter-than-life photo-art has been brought to bear on many famous faces, from Catherine Deneuve to Kylie Minogue. Their work has been featured in advertising (Absolut vodka, Britvic orange juice to name but two) and on numerous album covers. The male nude is one of Pierre et Gilles' fortés. Drawing on the imagery of early photographic pioneers like Wilhelm von Gloeden, as well as religious 'martyr' symbolism, few artists have captured the fantasy and perfection of male beauty quite like these two, as their exhaustive book *Pierre et Gilles* (Taschen) testifies.

JACK PIERSON

Bodies take on the warm glow of possibility in a Jack Pierson photograph. Soft light and a perspective defined by the focussed parts of the image are something of a signature for this New York-based multi-media artist and photographer. Often holed up in what may be hotels, or other people's bedrooms; sometimes in close-up, sometimes a little blurred, Pierson's 1950s Technicolor-like men are not grim reportage images of hustlers and bad boys, but filmic, fantasy figures that could be anything you want them to be – just like real life. He recently told *iD* magazine: "These images are more of a fiction than they are diaristic; but diaries are often fictions too...."

GEORGE PLATT LYNES (1907-1955)

Probably the most prolific male nude photographer of his time, and posthumously the most influential, George Platt Lynes was the pioneer of modern male nude photography. His fusion of the classic elements of fashion and portrait photography with the male figure brought a freshness and vitality to a genre that had largely been restricted to the subterfuge of 'physique' and 'naturist' styling. Platt Lynes' main career though, was in fashion and portraiture; very little of his male nude work was seen in his lifetime. His influence can be seen in the work of modern photographers like Robert Mapplethorpe and Bruce Weber.

HOUSK RANDALL-GODDARD

This hard-working, London-based Californian once described what he does as anthropology, and looking through his body of work you can see why. Housk Randall-Goddard has been cataloguing the real people on the UK fetish and body art scene since he came across this fascinating group in the late 1980s. His early work combined photography and watercolours to give these portraits a painterly feel. Later, he began a project to photograph friends from the scene nude and in their favourite fetishwear, which became the book *Revelations* (TWP). Further books included *Rituals of Love* (Picador) on SM couples and *The Customised Body* (Serpent's Tail).

TERRY RICHARDSON

One of the most exciting talents to come out of the world of fashion photography, and undoubtedly one of the most fearless, is Terry Richardson. His bold fashion and music images have been at the forefront of the new, game-on visual frontier, appearing regularly in the world's top style press. Richardson's images are graphic – very graphic: Batman and Robin having sex, VWE (very well endowed) young men on stained mattresses... you get the picture. Richardson, for all his style-mag credentials, is not afraid of the idea of shooting what it really means to get down and dirty – even if that means the less-than-endearing male habit of not cleaning your flat for weeks!

HERB RITTS

One of the best known, and loved, fashion and portrait photographers of the 1980s and '90s, Herb Ritts has been responsible for some of the most iconographic images in the history of photography. His work for *Vogue, Vanity Fair, Rolling Stone* magazine, Madonna, Calvin Klein, Giorgio Armani and Donna Karan, and his intelligent, characterful movie and rock star portraits have ensured Ritts's work has crossed over from cognoscenti to mass recognition. His clean, graphic figures, particularly his nude work, capture the emerging strength and liberated spirit of our age; his attention to detail – pin-sharp textures and contrasts – heightens the sensuality of his images. No anthology would be complete without this LA-based photographer.

HOWARD ROFFMAN

Photography is a labour of love more than a living for Howard Roffman, though this in no way diminishes this man's talent – far from it. This San Francisco-based executive with Lucas films recently told *Blue* magazine that he finds creating images outside the commercial world allows him to be "very pure with my art". Roffman came to prominence with his *Three* series – a hugely popular book, video and calendar of John, Gary and Kris, three men in a long-term relationship with each other. The trio became a hot talking point, as men debated the workability of multiple partnerships. Roffman followed up the success of *Three* with his new anthology, *Edge of Desire*.

RICHARD SAWDON SMITH

Winner of the John Kobal Photographic Portrait Award 1997, Richard Sawdon Smith's beautiful photographic work, based mostly around the male form, examines issues of sexuality, gender, HIV and AIDS (though most of these images are light hearted). This widely published London-based photographer mostly uses friends and acquaintances from the London scene, particularly the club Heaven, where he once worked as a photographer and dancer. Sawdon Smith is currently putting together a retrospective of his work with platinum printer Paul Cafell; a self-portrait which uses this special process can be seen in this book.

GUIDO SCHLINKERT

This Rome-based photographer began his artistic career in fine art and sculpture, occasionally incorporating photographs into his installations, exhibiting throughout Europe since 1985. For the past three years, he has been concentrating on his photography, though the artist's eye for movement and for charged forms is still very much evident in his stunning images of the male nude. Movement plays a large part in the magic of these pictures – the promise of some sensuous narrative is suggested by the blur of the naked figures in these dusty old Italian rooms. Roman classicism given a thoroughly modern twist.

LEEANNE SCHMIDT

Underwater love seems to be the driving force behind much of this Cincinnati-based photographer's work. Shooting the movement of light and shapes that her models make on the water in a bathtub set up in her backyard, Schmidt has created a series of beautifully fluid portraits. It is as if Schmidt is returning the human form back to the water it rose from. "For me, water is a metaphor for emotions and feelings," said Schmidt in a recent interview. "I use water as a tool to create a visual equivalent of the way humans distort and change their lives through feelings and actions."

STANLEY STELLAR

"To me, nudity is contrast. When you are nude, you are vulnerable. But you are also exposing your light. I oftentimes see the nude body as the light in contrast to darkness. So there's spirituality there, I guess." So said shining talent Stanley Stellar to US art photography magazine *Provocateur*. There's something about the way that a Stellar image glows out of the page that turns every figure shot by this internationally acclaimed, New York-based photographer into both everyman and superman. Stellar's combination of strength and vulnerability make a valuable contribution to the new wave of masculinity.

ROBERT TAYLOR

"My main preoccupations in photography are personal politics and pleasure. I am particularly interested in difference and the possibility that the distinctions that can be drawn between people are as exciting as they are threatening." So says Robert Taylor, a former barrister and member of the RAF, whose beautiful images embrace that thesis and run with it. Taylor's portrait and figure work has found its way into a wide range of arenas, from Peter Tatchell's groundbreaking Safer Sexy illustrated safe sex guidebook for gay men to the works bought by the National Portrait Gallery and the Victoria and Albert museum in London.

WOLFGANG TILLMANS

There is a zingy freshness about the photography of Wolfgang Tillmans that goes beyond mere use of colour. What may seem at first glance an eclectic, snapshot-style body of work, builds up through the artist's selection of images into an enlightening vision of the modern world as we actually experience it, a kaleidoscope of eating, sleeping, indoors, outdoors, friends, lovers, trains, pavement, sky – images that bounce between the exceptional and the banal, making everything fresh again. Selecting images from Tillmans' portfolio for this anthology continues this process by moving the gaze on to Tillmans' men – at home, in the street, in the great outdoors. A new way of seeing.

TRADE MARK

One of the most striking and most popular artists on London's club/art scene, we are stretching a point by including this dazzling illustrator in our photographic anthology, but it would be a poorer publication without Trade Mark's bold, brazen, beautiful men to lead the charge of the bright brigade. Coming to prominence as the club flyer illustrator of the early 'nineties, Trade Mark's work evolved from the seminal images he produced for the club that gave him his name. His work has since been used prolifically in magazines and advertising and exhibited all over the world. Strength through celebration seems to be the underlying theme of this currently London-based disco revolutionary.

DAVID VANCE

David Vance is a player in the high rolling world of photography. He enjoys a successful career in advertising and editorial, with assignments for many top magazines, from *Rolling Stone* to *Uomo Vogue* and clients like Sony, Miramax films and Coca-Cola. But it is his stunning male nude work which interests us here. Working out of his hometown, Miami, Vance makes full use of the bright natural light and stunning locations, to present the male figure to its fullest potential, as can be seen on our cover shot. Sunshine on their shoulders makes us happy. Books include *The Woods* (Pohlman Press) and *David Vance/Photographs* (Bruno Ghunder).

DEL LAGRACE VOLCANO

An American based in London, Del LaGrace Volcano, formerly known as Della Grace, first came to prominence in the early 'nineties through the striking images of the SM dyke scene published in this self-described pansexual's seminal photography book debut, Love Bites (GMP). LaGrace Volcano's work has gone on to celebrate many aspects of human sexuality and strength beyond the narrow definitions of gender and sexuality, including drag kings, lesbian boys and all shades in between, as seen in her latest publication, The Drag King Book (Serpent's Tail).

ANDY WARHOL (1930-87)

Along with his famous soup cans and celebrity portraits, during the late 'sixties, Andy Warhol also shot a series of male nudes, often using the newly available Polaroid film. Mainly concentrating on close-ups of the torso, some of these images were later transformed into paintings, others went on exhibition untouched. Rumour has it that after taking these images (some of which are much more explicit and 'pronounced' than the ones featured in this anthology), Mr Warhol needed to sit down and calm himself. Who said Pop Art was easy?

TREVOR WATSON

This hard-working London-based photographer is one of the best-known and loved names in the world of fetish and erotic art. Watson's work covers a wide range of styles, from fashion to hardcore; when it comes to capturing a strong image, this man knows no fear, no genre boundaries. Specialising in black and white images, though sometimes treated with colour in post-production/Photoshop, Watson's work often has an edge to it that takes it beyond mere glamour posturing and into the realms of art, though the wicked Watson sense of humour is never far away.

HYWEL WILLIAMS

Like many contributors to this anthology, Hywel Williams came to photography after an early career change – in his case, from teaching. After studying photography in Manchester, this Liverpool-based Welshman moved to London in 1969 and began working in commercial photography and in various printing darkrooms. Williams became a freelance photographer in 1988. In 1990 the Gay Men's Press published a beautiful book of his colour work. He has been actively involved in the media campaign around the AIDS issue, donating images to the Gay Men Fighting AIDS campaign. Asked what his ambitions are now, this modest man laughingly replies: "With cigarette in my hand – to live for another twelve months."

DAVID ZANES

This top fashion photographer began shooting nudes about five years ago as a way of trying out new technical and artistic ideas outside of his commissioned work. The images chosen for this anthology are taken from a much larger collection and include several techniques that this New York-born, London-based photographer employs to great effect, including body paint, Polaroid image transfers and double exposures. Lucky us – this is the first time this beautiful work has been published, though Zanes is currently considering publishing more of his exquisite nude work. He can be reached at DAZphoto@aol.com.

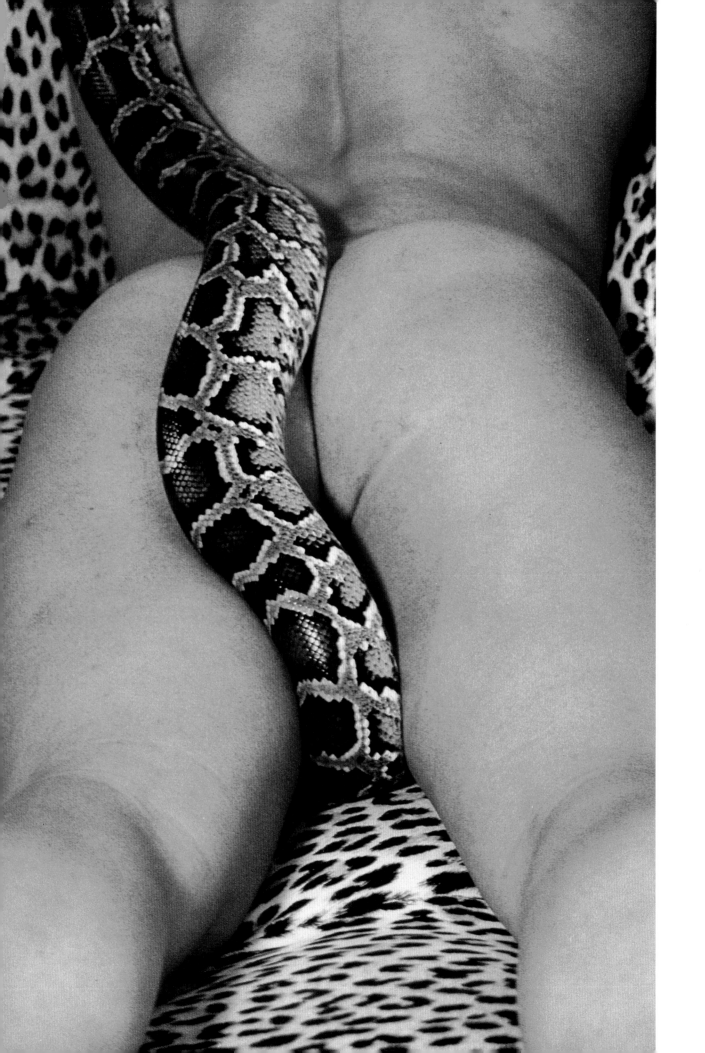

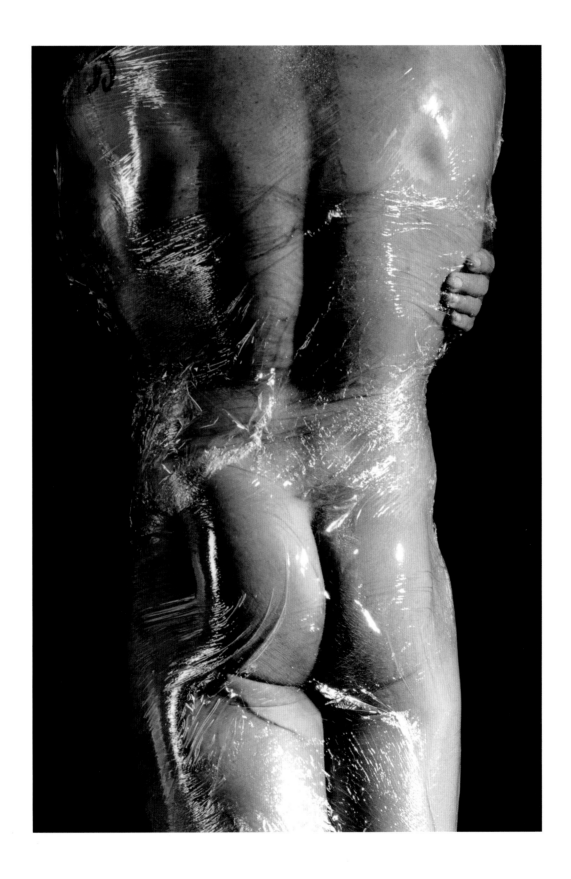

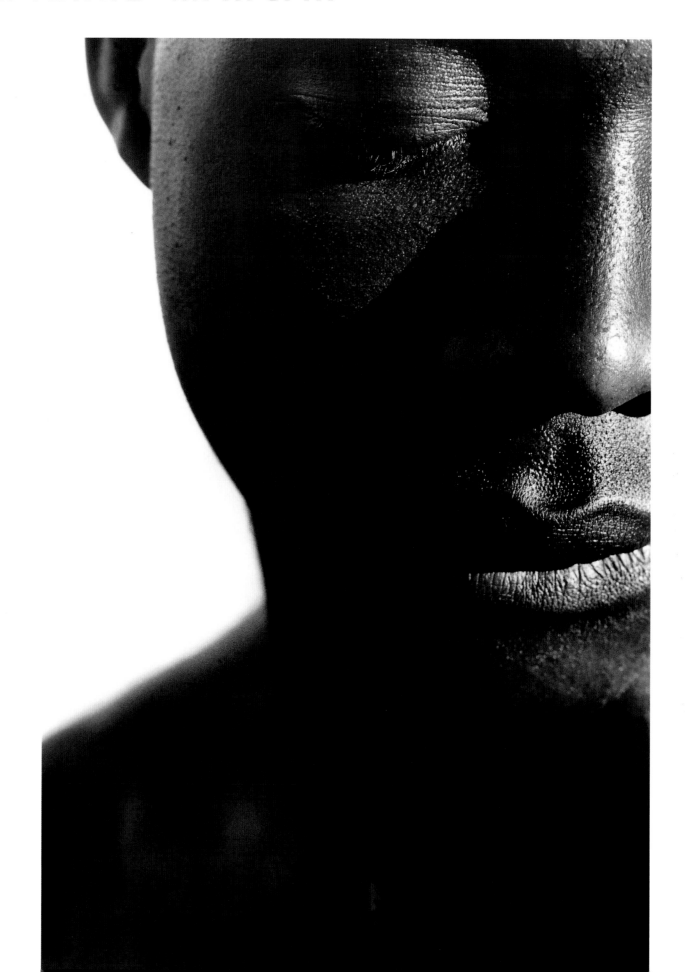

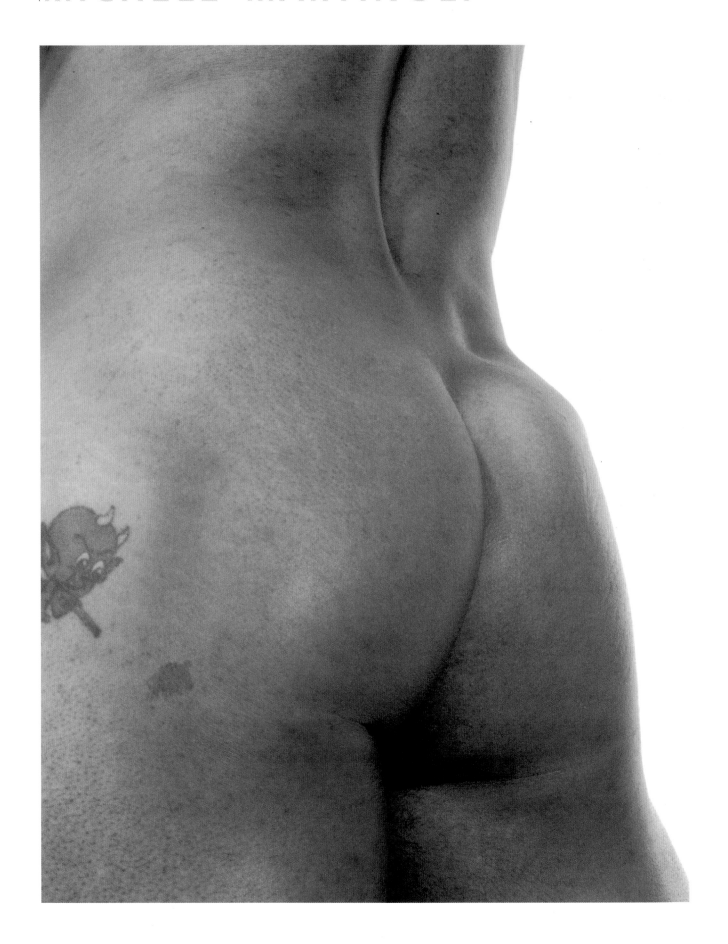

DAVID MORGAN

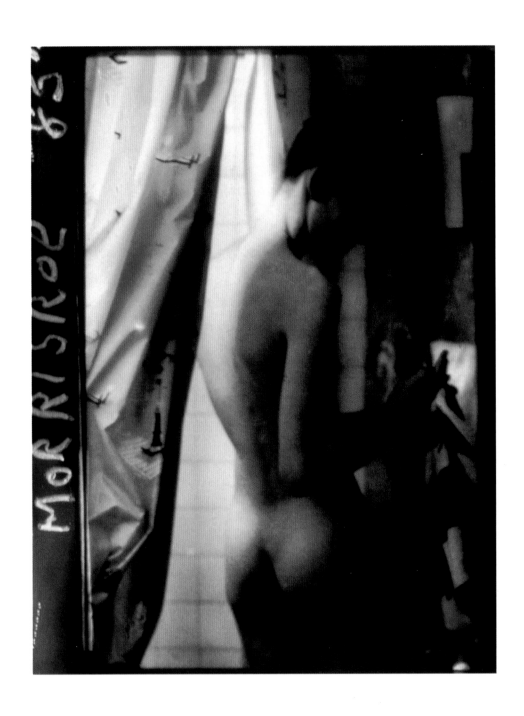

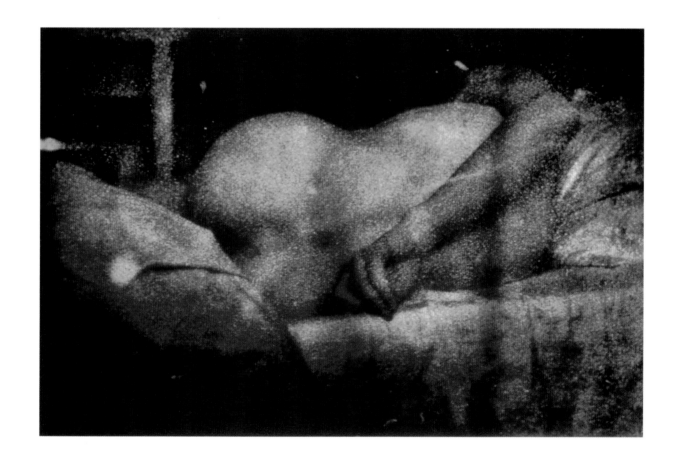

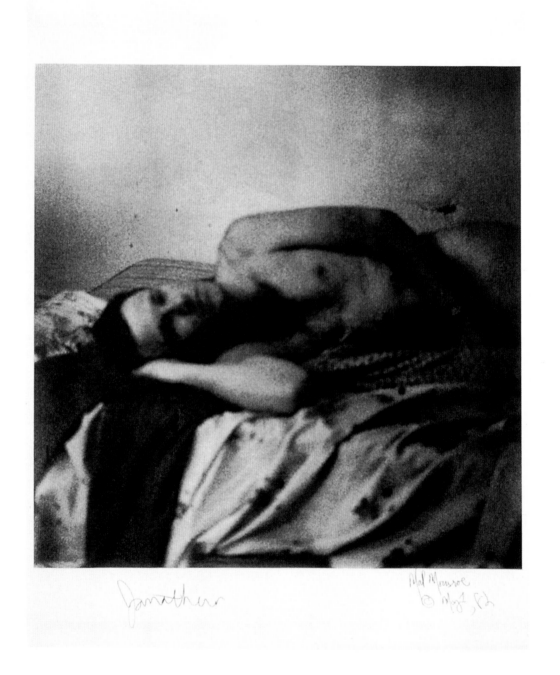

Jonathan   Mark Morrisroe
                                            © 1987 82

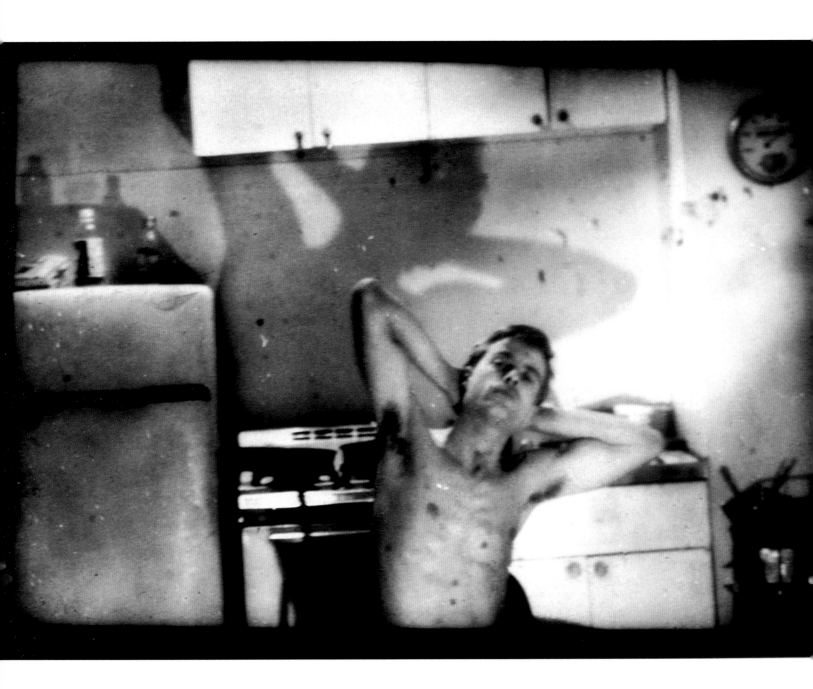

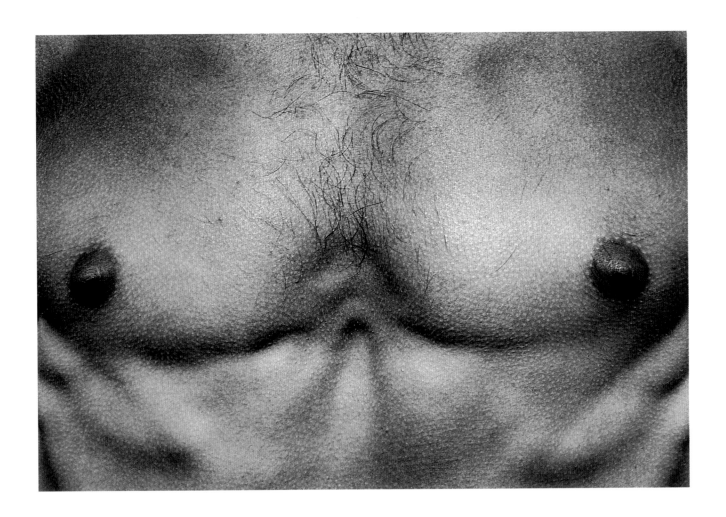

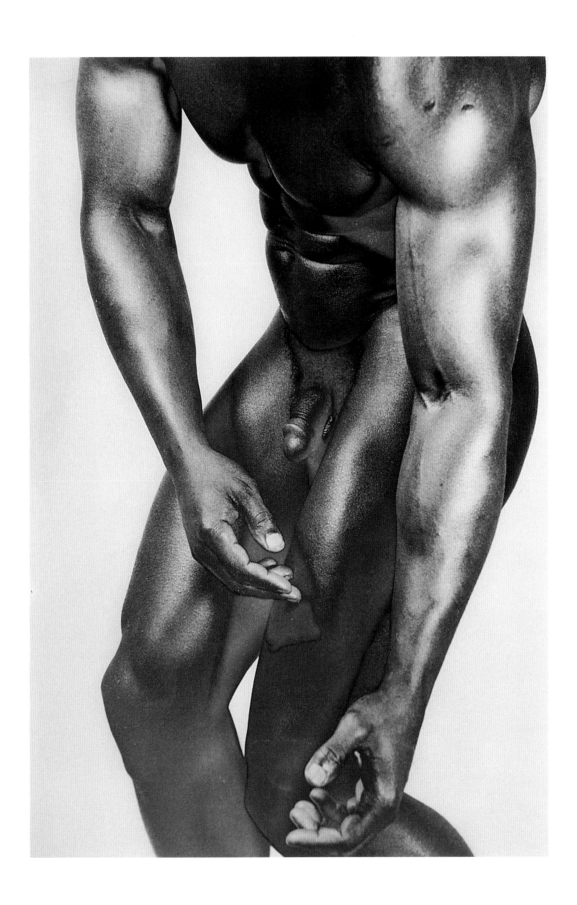

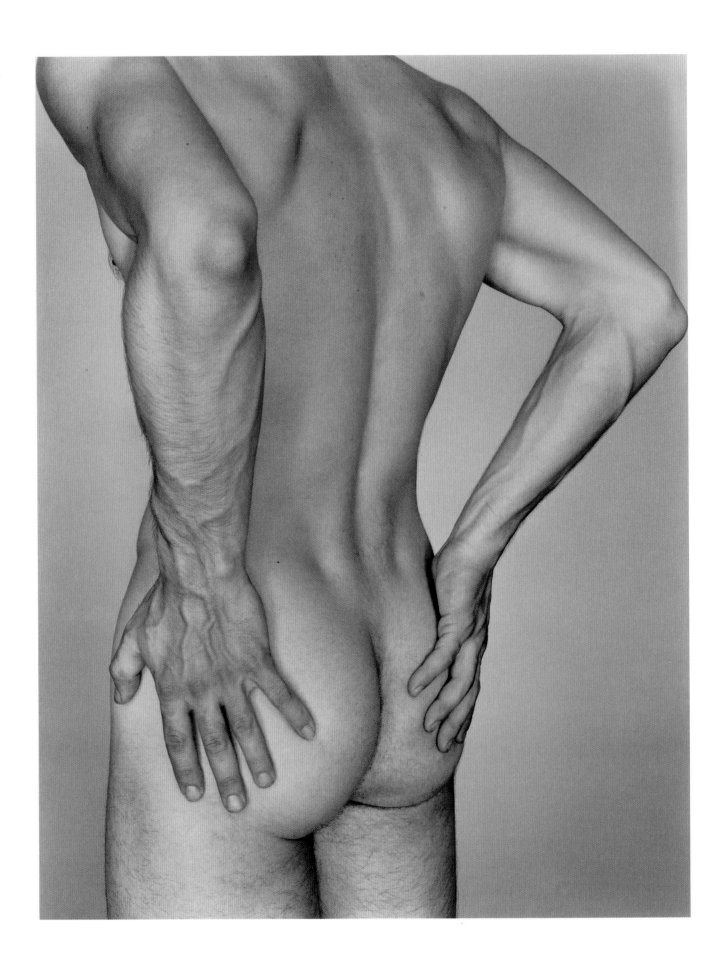

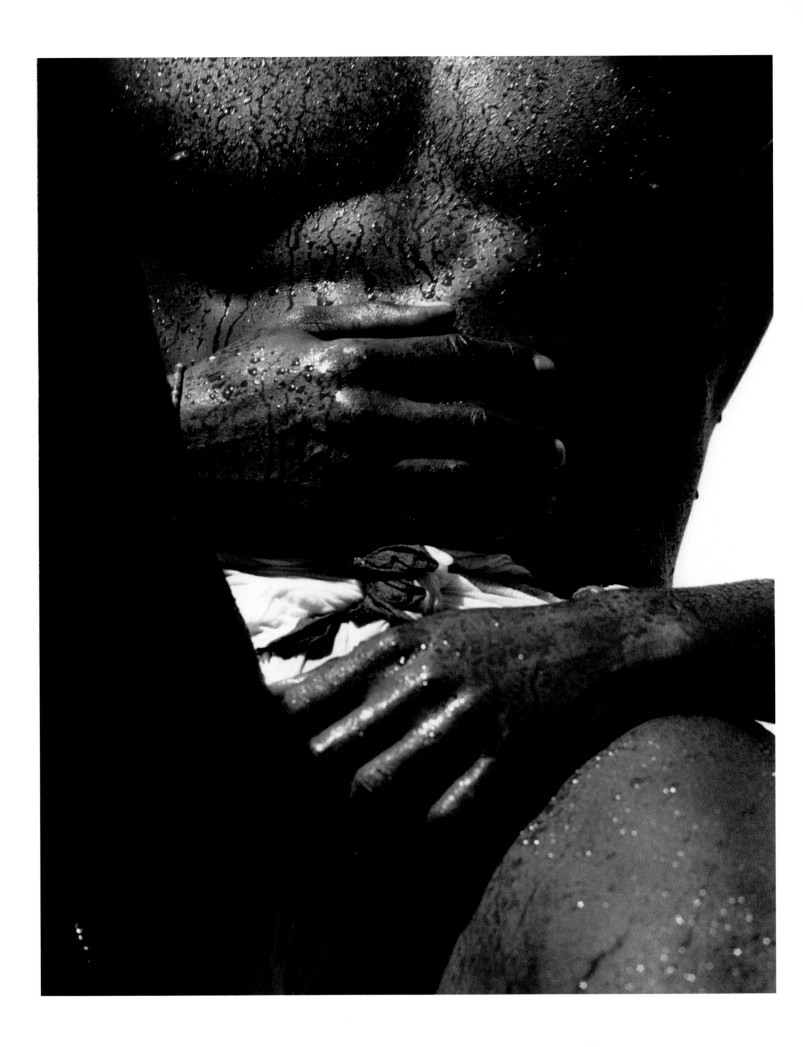

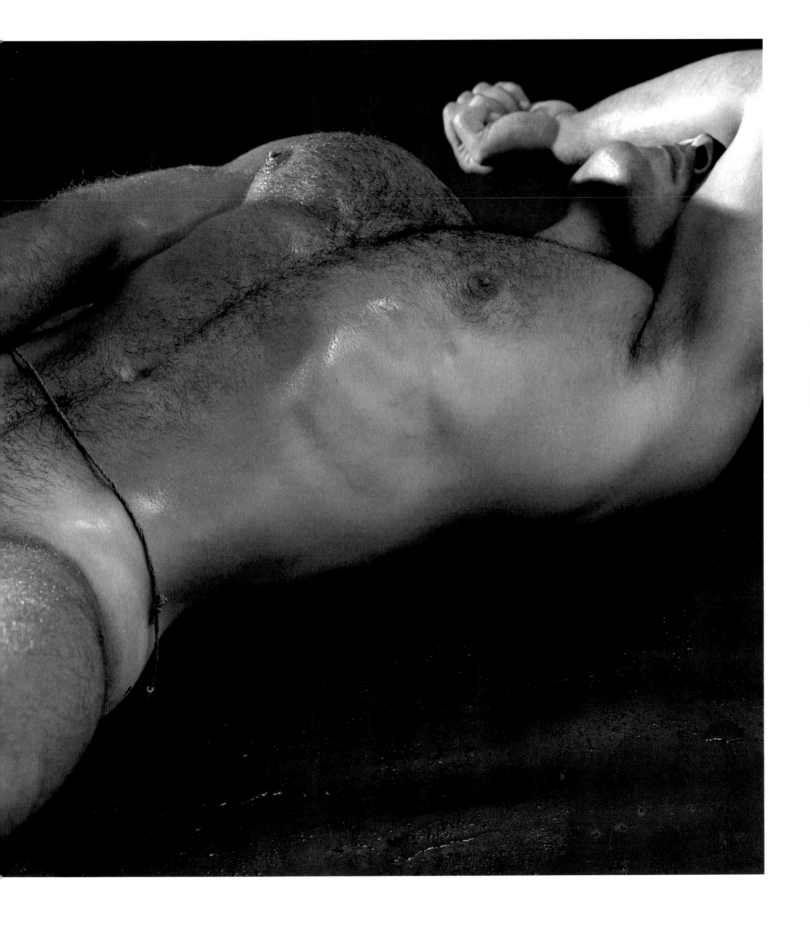

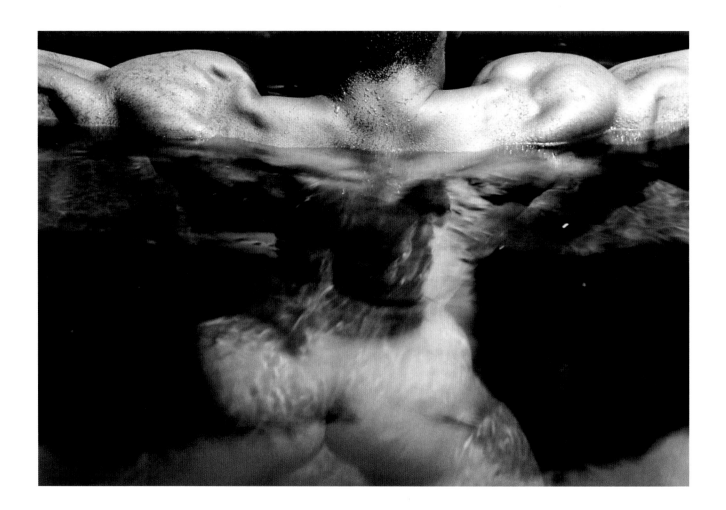

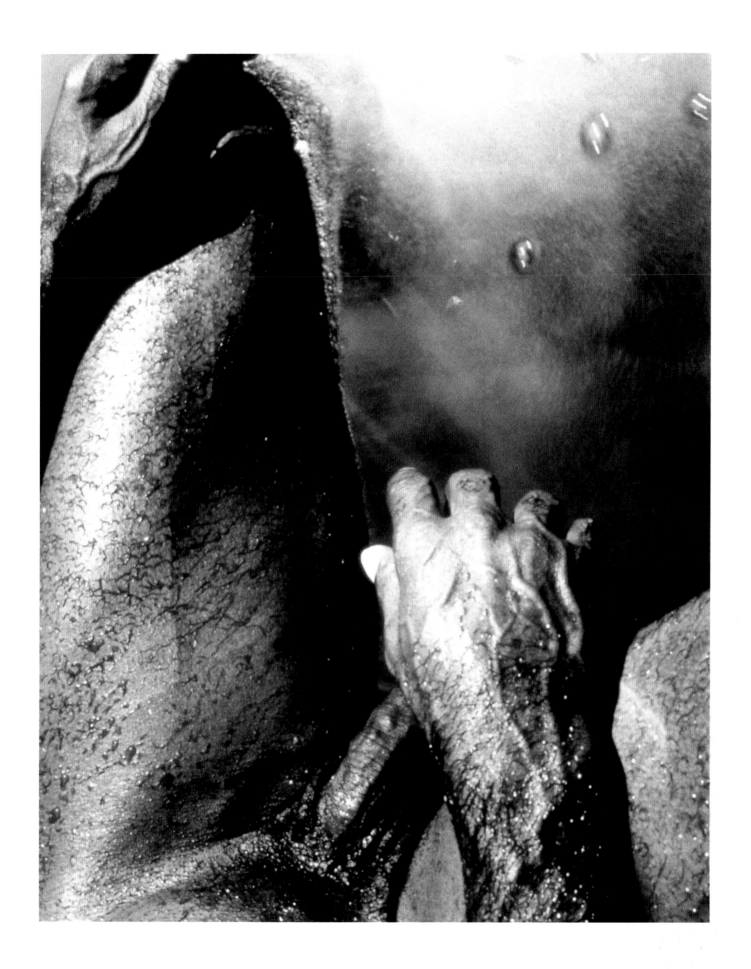

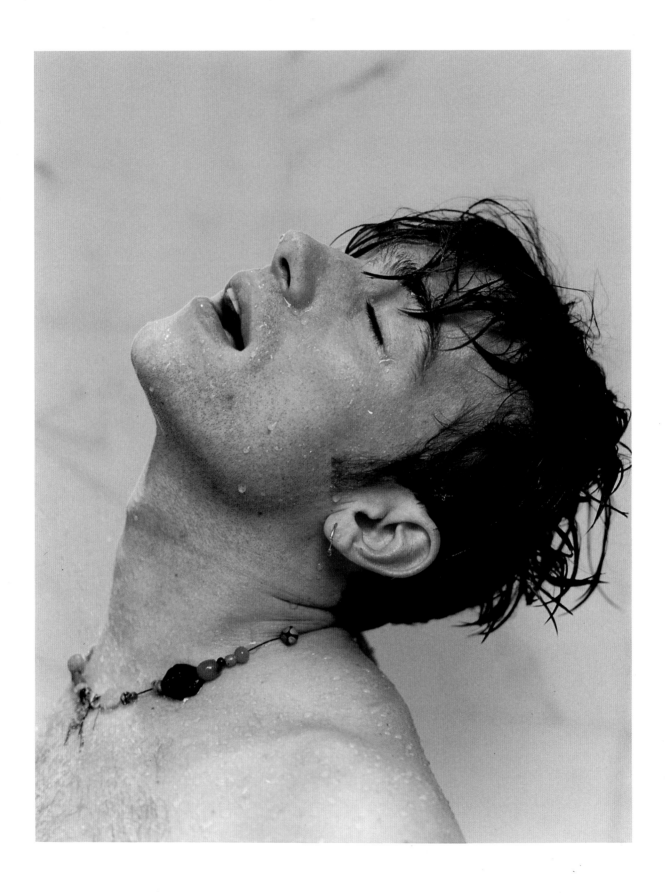

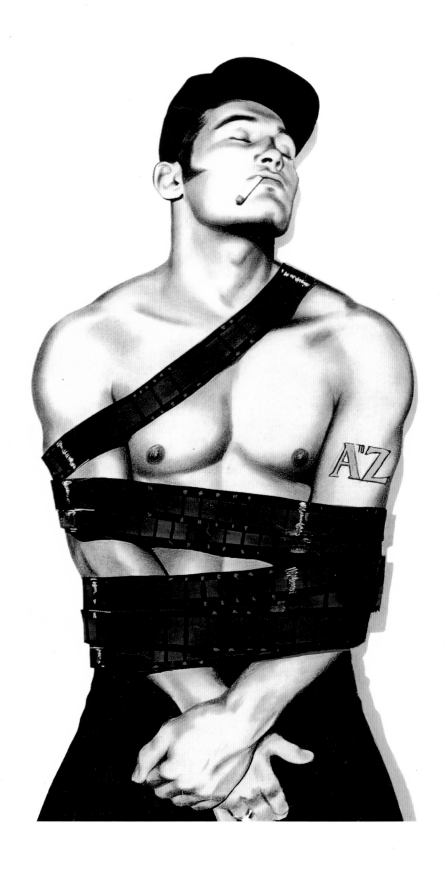

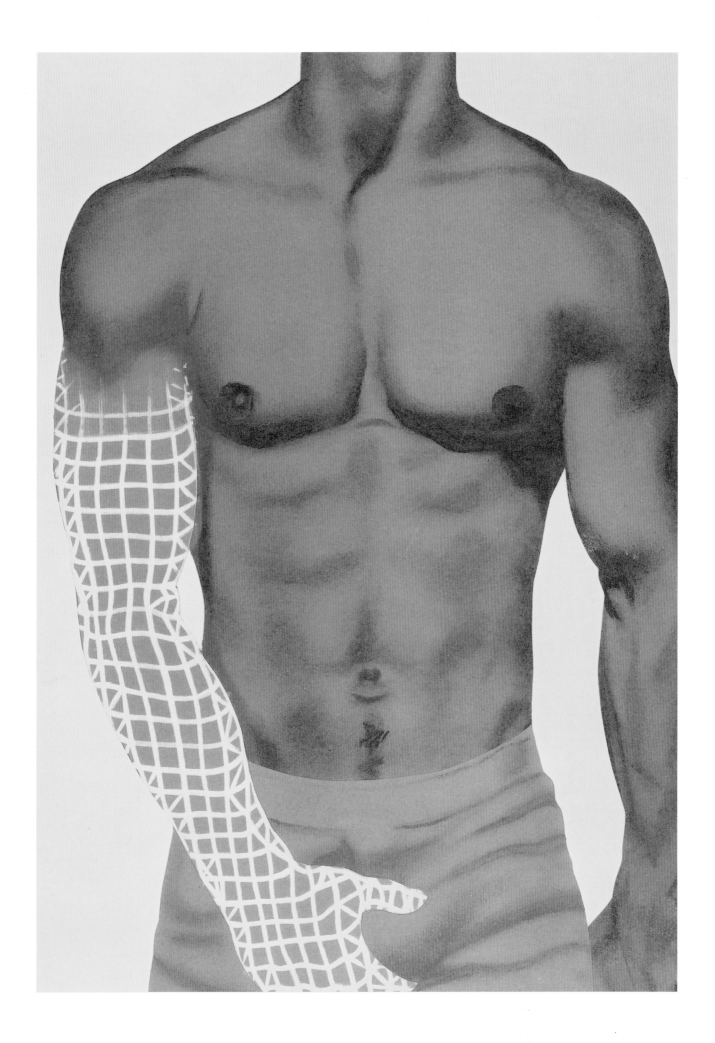

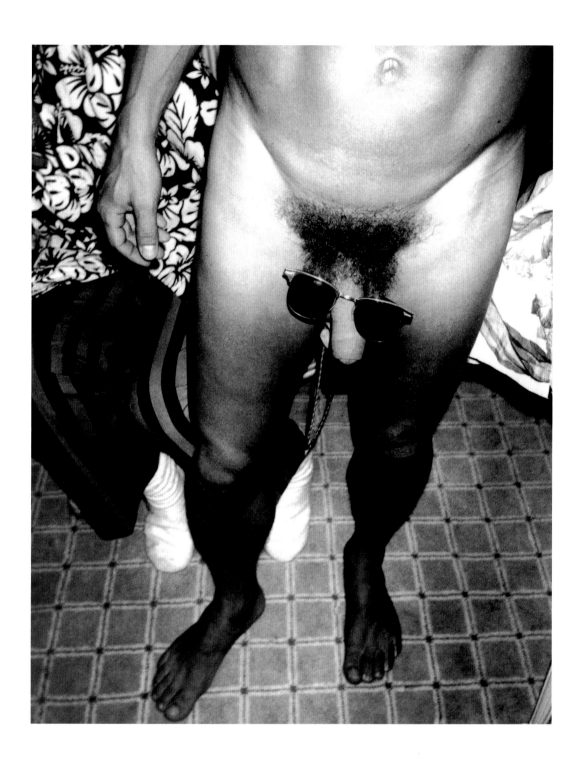

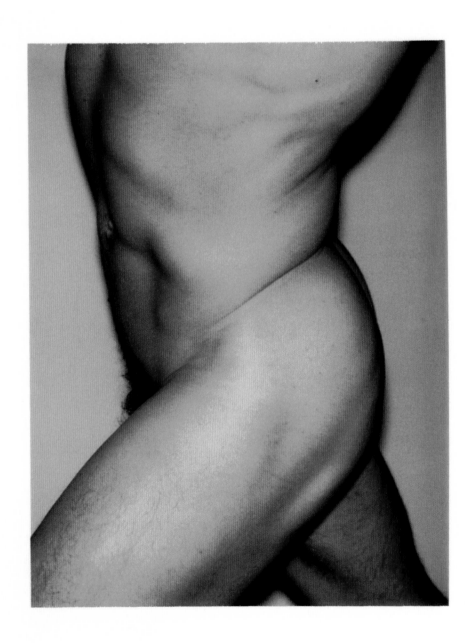

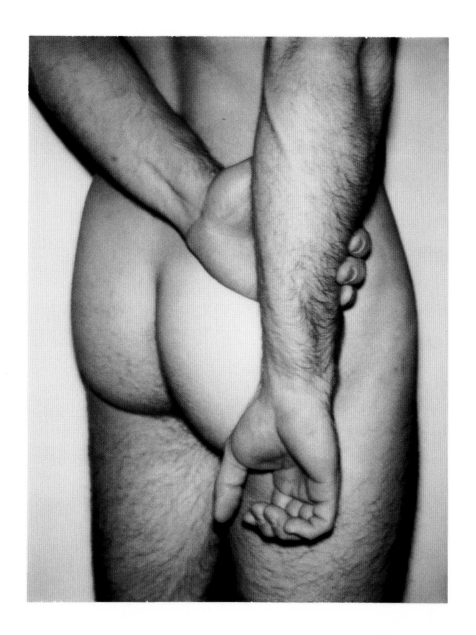

PICTURE ACKNOWLEDGEMENTS

Carlton Books would like to extend a special thank you to all the photographers for their help and co-operation in this project.

THANK YOU ALSO TO:
David Leddick for helping source George Platt Lynes, David Zanes
(DAZphoto@aol.com), Kerri at Visages Syndication for Herb Ritts, Uwe Scheid
Collection for Wilhelm von Gloeden, Leigh and Tracy at Hamiltons for Horst P.
Horst, John Wascinsin for Howard Roffman

ADDITIONAL PICTURE CREDITS:
Ian David Baker/GAZE International 40-43
Robert Flynt courtesy of Robert Flynt and Vance Martin Photography and Fine
Art, San Francisco 50-53
Wilhelm von Gloeden, courtesy of Uwe Scheid Collection 56-59
Baly Hinter Wipflinger, courtesy of GAZE International, London 72-75
Horst P. Horst, courtesy of Hamiltons, London 76-79
Sandra Jensen, Black Factory Studio 86-87
Estate of Mark Morrisroe, courtesy of Pat Hearn Gallery, NY 126-128
Pierre & Gilles; courtesy of Yannick Morisot, Paris 142-149
George Platt Lynes, courtesy of David Leddick in Miami, Wilbur Pippin in
Conneticut and George Platt Lynes II 154-159
Terry Richardson, courtesy of Katy Barker Agency, London 164-165
Herb Ritts, courtesy of Visages, Los Angeles 166-167
Howard Roffman; courtesy of John Wascisin 168-173
Guido Schlinkert, courtesy of Il Ponte Contemporanea, Rome 178-183
Leeanne Schmidt, courtesy of Gallery 292, New York 184-187
Robert Taylor, courtesy of GAZE International, London 190-191
The Andy Warhol Foundation, Inc./Art Resource, NY 206-209
Hywel Williams/GAZE International, London 216-217

Every effort has been made to acknowledge correctly and contact the source and/or copyright holder of
each picture, and Carlton Books Limited apologizes for any unintentional errors or omissions which will
be corrected in future editions of this book.